Steam Memorires on Shed: 1950's – 1960's

No. 40: Glasgow Engine S

D Dunn

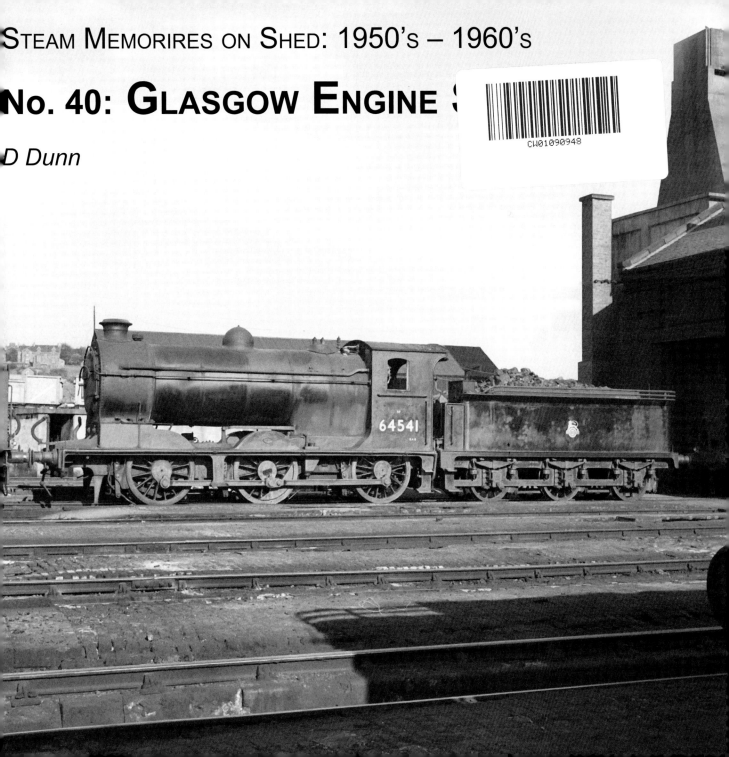

Copyright Book Law Publications 2012

ISBN 978-1-907094-70-5

INTRODUCTION

The engine sheds on the north bank of the Clyde around Glasgow which under BR became part of the 65 District under Eastfield were a diverse lot which originally belonged to two of the 'Big Four' companies and, even earlier than that, belonged to Scotland's two major railways – the Caledonian and the North British. British Railways added to the diversification by making the district rather larger than originally intended by introducing the former Caley shed at Grangemouth, and the ex-NBR shed at Fort William, into the mix. So from a concentration of depots around the north of Glasgow, we spread out to the west coast, and virtually the east coast!

Not all of the engine sheds within what became the 65 District are covered in this album; space did not permit the inclusion of 300 plus illustrations. So, what have we got: Eastfield because of what it was and its position in the hierarchy; St Rollox (Balornock) likewise; Parkhead, Dawsholm, Kipps and Grangemouth are also included. The smaller sheds, Balloch, Helensbugh, Yoker are not featured, this time! But, going out, on a limb, literally, we have brought Fort William into the fold just as BR did between 1955 and 1960. Hopefully this mixture will be to your liking as will the combination of what was then old and new. The comparison between Kipps and Fort William are striking.

Acknowledgements: We would like to thank Richard Strange, of the *What Really Happened To Steam* group, who solved the mystery – to us – of why No.46227 was stabled at Eastfield on 2nd November 1963. Also, thanks to Ian Trivett for information on a certain piece of rolling stock which became a fixture at Eastfield.

Cover Picture
Ex-works resident K2 No.61788 LOCH RANNOCH stands on No.6 road at the south end of Eastfield shed on Saturday 8th September 1956. Note the double lining afforded to the cylinders. *C.J.B.Sanderson.*

Previous Page
Resident J37 No.64541 rests at sunset at the north end of Eastfield engine shed in September 1956. *C.J.B.Sanderson.*

Printed and bound by The Amadeus Press, Cleckheaton, West Yorkshire
First published in the United Kingdom by Book Law Publications, 382 Carlton Hill, Nottingham, NG4 1JA

The north yard of Eastfield engine shed on Saturday 29th April 1950 with an assortment of classes, livery styles, ages, and coal quality! Some former LNER numbering is still prominent nearly two years and four months after the demise of that company: J37 No.4601 and Q1 No.9925 being the chief candidates, the latter even managing to keep hold of the cast, and rather attractive, LNER totem plate on the bunker (both of the Scottish, Eastfield based Q1s – 69925 and 69927 – actually managed to keep hold of their cast totem plates until withdrawal on 13th August 1954 and 18th April 1956 respectively). Nearly another year would pass before the Q1 got its BR identity whereas the J37 had only five months to wait for its repaint and renumbering. Four WD 'Austerity' 2-8-0s are present though only No.90174 with its number painted on the smokebox can be identified. A brand new B1, ex NBL Co. – that would be No.61367 which was released to BR the day before – bound for Colwick. No.61368, which was also headed for Nottinghamshire, was released on Sunday 30th April so they may well have travelled south together. Note that all the tenders and bunkers are topped-up ready for Monday's tasks. At this date the engine shed has all of its ventilators, one over each road, at least on this section of the transverse roof. *C.J.B.Sanderson.*

The east side of the north yard at Eastfield on the first full day of the ASLEF strike – 29th May 1955 – with all the engines coaled-up but all the fires dropped! A vision of the future, perhaps, with lines of dead locomotives waiting for the call to the scrap yard! However, this lot were far from finished and were only waiting for the strike to be called off. In all, some seventeen days would elapse before things got moving again and the locomotives went back to work. How long it took to light all the fires and get the boilers up to pressure is unknown but it wouldn't have been overnight. This aspect of the shed was captured from the railway bridge (which features in so many photographs taken at Eastfield shed) which crossed the yard at its north end and which carried a former Caledonian goods line known as the Hamiltonhill branch. *F.W.Hampson.*

The view across the north yard at Eastfield shed on the evening of the first day of the 1955 Strike, looking from west to east. An enthusiasts dream is revealed but that same aspect would have been a traveller's nightmare. Remember that this was just one engine shed; there were hundreds like this all over the country for more than two weeks. This view enables us to look at the shed itself in relation to the coaling plant. The redundant coaling stage, actually kept in situ for the last twenty-odd years or so in case the mechanical plant should break down – a catastrophic event at a depot such as Eastfield without a back-up. It would be interesting to know the numbers of the locomotives on shed on this particular day and for the following seventeen days too. The three illustrations featured reveal just a few of the actual locomotive numbers. *F.W.Hampson.*

D30 No.62429 THE ABBOT is prominent in this close-up of the north yard on that 29th day of May 1955. Note the differing qualities of coal in the tenders; it appears to vary from mediocre to dusty slack. The latter was the type of coal which would have been discarded onto a mine's spoil heap in pre-war days but by 1955 it was increasingly becoming the norm for mixed traffic and goods engines on BR as mechanisation underground was bringing out a greater tonnage of coal but at a cost in quality. *F.W.Hampson.*

Just over a year previous to our dramatic 1955 scenes, on Saturday 17th April 1954, we have this different aspect of the north yard of the shed which reveals the fourteen-road building in its entirety though not with as many locomotives in view; those which are on show are in steam too. N15 No.69218 makes its way to the 70ft turntable after visiting the coaling plant. When it had completed its turn ready for Monday morning's duty, the 0-6-2T would retire to a designated shed road for the weekend. Note that the shed was bereft of smoke ventilators at this side of the roof. *C.J.B.Sanderson.*

One of Dunfermline's J88s, No.68351, hides between the east wall of the main shed and the oil store at the south end of the shed on 17th April 1954. Notice that even by this day, the 0-6-0T still displays its former owner's initials more than six years after the LNER ceased to exist. More to the point, what was this engine doing at Eastfield shed other than waiting to visit Cowlairs works? The diminutive tank was in fact waiting to enter Cowlairs and which it duly did on the following Tuesday, for a General overhaul lasting some three and a half weeks. During that time No.68351 received a new boiler, attention to other worn out parts and of course a repaint complete with the application of the BR lion and wheel emblem. Besides the dumb buffers carried by this class, note also the absence of a coupling hook on the beam; obviously they couldn't haul each other around! The pile of bricks stacked against the shed wall is evidence of the brick arch renewals carried out at sheds such as this. As for the amount of lubricating oil issued each day, it doesn't bare thinking about but those 40-gallon drums didn't last too long once opened. *C.J.B.Sanderson.*

8

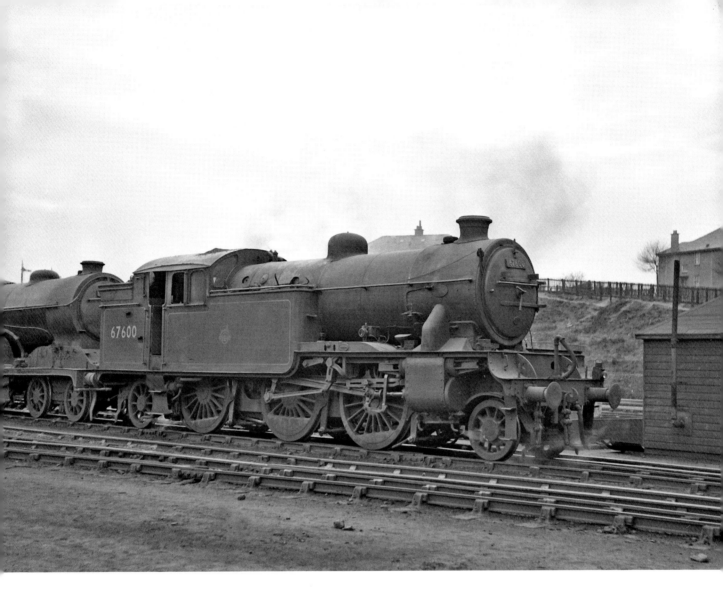

Eastfield shed was home for the engines used for banking the passenger trains out of Glasgow (Queen Street) and up the Cowlairs incline. Over the years since the station was opened, not including the period when rope haulage was the mode, numerous classes have been tried and used at length including the Gresley V1. This is No.67600 on 17th April 1954 on shed at Eastfield and showing the cable connection between the cab and the slip coupling; the pulley on the front edge of the smokebox is prominent. This V1 spent all of its life, barring a two month period in the summer of 1948, allocated to Eastfield shed and was equipped to bank trains out of Queen Street from June 1953, taking the place of the N15s which had been used beforehand. Seven other members of the class – Nos.67601, 67603, 67608, 67628, 67664, 67671 and 67680 – are known to have been similarly fitted for the duty during the same period of the mid-1950s. *C.J.B.Sanderson.*

In April 1954 it was still possible to see this Edinburgh & Glasgow Railway milepost at Eastfield shed. The E&G, which began services between the two cities in 1842 (Queen St. – Haymarket), was absorbed into the North British Railway in 1865 so this relic of the past, which was still giving up-to-date information, had done well in the best of Scottish traditions! *C.J.B.Sanderson.*

On a glorious summer Saturday, recently ex works J88 No.68340 (General overhaul at Cowlairs 18th to 29th May) from St Margarets shed, brightens up an already bright sunny morning at Eastfield shed on 5th June 1954. The location is the south yard looking north-east towards the coaling plant and the No.14 road of the engine shed. A couple of former LMS locomotives appear to be gracing the shed, a Stanier Class '5' on No.13 road; a total of twenty-two different Cl.5s were allocated to Eastfield shed at different periods from February 1950 onwards. Three of those did two stints. The longest residency was more than eight years whilst the shortest was just three months when No.44970 arrived for its second period in June 1965 but was then withdrawn during September. They were favourites on the West Highland. The other ex-LMS engine, stabled near the oil store, was a 'Crab' which must have been a visitor from any one of the eleven Scottish Region sheds which had one or more allocated at this time – Eastfield never had one of the 2-6-0s allocated. Note that at this end of the shed building ventilators, albeit of two very distinct types, still grace the roof. *C.J.B.Sanderson.*

Corkerhill 2P No.40649 was just ex Cowlairs works (the previous Friday afternoon) when this nice broadside view was recorded at the north end of the shed on Saturday 5th June 1954. The paint finish is a credit to the Cowlairs painters – another view of this engine on the same day but from a different angle reveals a mirror-like finish to exhibition standards – but that's how they turned them out, every time! The 4-4-0 had entered Cowlairs for stripping on Wednesday 5th May and was turned out after a 'General' on the 4th June. In stark contrast and immediately behind is the filthy WD 2-10-0, No.90751, which had not been cleaned since it was last in works nearly a year before, during June and July 1953. Three roads further west an unidentified B1 has also just been released from Cowlairs and is painted to the same standard as the 2P. *C.J.B.Sanderson.*

Another near exhibition finish is displayed by N15 No.69155 stabled with another N15, No.69178, one of Eastfield's own, on Saturday 6th April 1957. This Carlisle Canal based 0-6-2T had been at Eastfield for exactly a week since being released by Cowlairs after attending for not only its final 'General' but also its last visit to works for repair. A refurbished boiler, along with a thorough overhaul, helped the N15 to keep going for another five years until withdrawn at the end of the summer timetable in 1962, aged fifty years exactly. After this final weekend at Eastfield, No.69155 would soon be heading home via Edinburgh and the Waverley route; old habits die hard. Being the recipient of so many ex-works locomotives from Cowlairs, Eastfield had a responsible job in checking and making sure that all was well before they sent them on their way to the home depots. The normal 'running-in' period was anything from a couple of days to a week; each class had their own idiosyncrasies and no two locomotives were the same anyway. Nevertheless Eastfield certainly had a couple or more clean locomotives to greet weekend visitors. No.69155 did make one last visit to Cowlairs, in June 1963, when it went in for breaking up. *C.J.B.Sanderson.*

Not all of the overhauled output from Cowlairs was treated to lining. Kingmoor based 4F 0-6-0 No.44181 was regarded at a goods engine and was not therefore entitled to refinements such as lining. This 6th April 1957 view of the 4F shows that it has probably been out of the shops for a couple of days or more, the staining and dust accumulating on the horizontal surfaces indicating a period in steam and some time on shed. *C.J.B.Sanderson.*

Kittybrewster B1 No.61347 is seen in July 1957 just about to leave the shed precincts on a typical early running-in turn, working a lightweight goods train, to make sure all the moving parts are doing just that; and that the fixed parts remain just so. Note also that the 4-6-0 has been treated to the Cowlairs speciality for this class – the flowing, and continuous curving lining from the front bufferbeam to the cab, the corner fillets at each end of the running plate being a Cowlairs fitment which enabled that finish to be attained. Other refinements visible include highlighting the front numberplate, applying the Classification on the front bufferbeam, along with the name of the home shed, as if the shedplate wasn't enough. Note that Cowlairs lined the cylinders of ex-LNER locomotives with single lining although the K2s were treated to double lining! The Gorton-built engine had just finished a 'General' (10th May to 15th June), its second and last, and was amongst the first BR locomotives to receive the new British Railways crest in place of the old 'lion and wheel' emblem. The crest on this side of the tender is correct in every detail but the transfer on the right side would have been incorrect in having a wrong right-facing lion. Enjoying a longer life than many of its sisters, No.61347 spent the whole of its life in Scottish Region and was finally withdrawn from Thornton Junction shed on 4th April 1967. *C.J.B.Sanderson.*

Although initially allocated to Yoker shed, North British Loco. Co. built 0-4-0 diesel hydraulic D2734 spent its first week on BR at Eastfield shed where shed staff were allowed to familiarise themselves with its internal workings and performance. Arriving from the makers on Friday 17th October 1958, the little 0-4-0DH still looks brand-new in this scene at the south end of Eastfield shed on Saturday 25th of that month. Standing on No.1 road, the shunter is now in an area of the shed designated for diesel use only. When Yoker shed actually received their new charge is unknown but once resident it stayed until transferred to St Rollox shed on 11th January 1964. Nearly two years later on 4th December 1965, it was re-allocated to Eastfield for its final eighteen months or so of work prior to withdrawal under the so-called National Traction Plan whereby all non-standard locomotives, shunting or main-line, were to be withdrawn. Being a diesel hydraulic, and also finding redundancy staring it in the face, D2734 was amongst the group destined for a short operational life. Withdrawal took place on 16th September 1967 and by December it was in the hands of a nearby scrap yard in Shettelston. Having been built in Glasgow, worked all of its nine years in and around the city, it was perhaps appropriate that its demise should take place there too. *C.J.B.Sanderson.*

Framed by the stanchions on either side of No.10 road, WD 'Austerity' No.90690 rests on No.9 road on Sunday 13th September 1959 after a visit to Cowlairs works. The Thornton Junction based 2-8-0 had arrived at Eastfield on the previous Friday afternoon after completing a Heavy Intermediate overhaul (9th August to 11th September); evidence of touch-up painting can be seen around the front end, otherwise the rest of the locomotive has simply been given a thorough clean. *C.J.B.Sanderson.*

'Clan' Pacific No.72007 CLAN MACKINTOSH blows off whilst traversing the turntable road at the north end of Eastfield's yard on 1st October 1960. Just ex-works, the Kingmoor Pacific had undergone its second and final boiler change during a General overhaul at Cowlairs. Note that the 'Clan' appears to have just visited the coaling plant, and having now turned, it is about to reverse onto the shed on this damp Saturday. Although under the care of Crewe initially, heavy maintenance of the 'Clans' passed to Cowlairs from April 1958 when no less than three of the class – 72006, 72007 and 72008 – attended the Glasgow works for heavy overhauls during that month. St Rollox had dealt with four of the class during 1956/57 but Cowlairs became responsible from 1958 until the demise of the class in 1966 although no major works attention was given to any of the class after 72009 received a 'General' in late 1962. It would be interesting to know the route taken by No.72007 to get back to Carlisle. *C.J.B.Sanderson.*

Another 'Standard', this time a rather grotty one in the shape of Stranraer's Cl.4 2-6-0 No.76112, lies dead on Eastfield's north yard on 1st October 1960 with its smokebox door slightly ajar, and a smokebox ash screen displaced outside on the front panel. A chalked message beneath the lower step of the running plate mentions a 'split pin out of .....'? It seems like a job for Cowlairs or has it already visited that works? The pony wheel looks suspiciously clean compared with the rest of the engine and that AWS appears recently fitted. The WD tender belongs to 2-10-0 No.90757 which had preceded the 'standard' from Cowlairs. One of thirty-five initially allocated to the Scottish Region, No.76112 was amongst the final batch of Doncaster's last five steam locomotives built at that workshop in late 1957. The Scottish Region was the first recipient of the class when Nos.76000 to 76004 arrived at Motherwell from Horwich in December 1952. Appropriately the last one built, No.76099, was also allocated to the Region, Corkerhill in fact, and that also came from Horwich, in November 1957. The Cl.4s ranged all over Scotland from Kittybrewster to Stranraer, the bulk of them being allocated to Glasgow area sheds. No.76112 went new to Dumfries in September 1957 but by the following Christmas had transferred to the west coast shed where it remained until withdrawn in October 1965. Note the enthusiastic but mistaken storage of coal on the cab roof – looks like a job for one of the shed cleaners on Monday morning! The coal incident seems to indicate that the Cl.4 has just returned from main works – engines entering shops usually had empty tenders. *C.J.B.Sanderson.*

Arriving on shed during Friday 30th September 1960, after completing an Intermediate repair at Cowlairs which started 25th August, Grangemouth based WD 2-10-0 No.90757 graces Eastfield's north yard with its massive presence on Saturday 1st October 1960. New cylinder covering and partial steam pipe covers appear to highlight the work undertaken at Cowlairs. The short career of these ten-coupled engines saw all twenty-five allocated to Scottish Region – trials and loans omitted – throughout their lives. Indeed this particular engine was subject to a number of trials in 1952 when it went on a near-countywide tour to show off its prowess, etc., to the motive power departments of the ER, SR and WR! Transferring to Grangemouth on 19th November 1949 after nine months at Carstairs depot, No.90757 (or 73781 as it was then until April 1950) settled down to what would become a thirteen year association with the shed interrupted only by that aforementioned three month excursion. That tour started at Doncaster on 9th August and over the following month the big engine spent various amounts of time at different sheds in the area, Frodingham for instance had its presence for about a week. Moving on to Banbury on 6th September, it was given short thrift by the Western Region and a week later it was on its way to Ashford. This latter shed knew the class quite well and had used them on and off to an extent since 1945 and on through to BR's adoption of the twenty-five Scottish engines. The Southern kept hold of the 2-10-0 for six weeks but it is not known if it was in continual use or spent periods in store. Following return to Grangemouth on 1st November, the WD continued where it had left off. Perhaps because Grangemouth housed the bulk of the class, most of the final fifteen active members, including No.90757, were withdrawn from that shed on 29th December 1962. *C.J.B.Sanderson.*

As mentioned earlier, Eastfield was home to a number of Stanier Cl.5s during the BR period and here on the wet ash pit at the rear – east side – of the shed on 6th September 1962 Nos.44787 and 44968 undergo servicing. It is worth listing, perhaps, the locomotives involved and the dates allocated to 65A which show an almost continuous presence of the class from February 1950 to September 1964 with just two short breaks in continuity during 1951 and 1953: 44702 – 3/57-12/62; 44707 – 10/55-1/63; 44787 – 5/55-12/62; 44791 – 2/50-8/50; 44908 – 3/52-8/53 & 1/58-12/62; 44921 – 8/51-5/52; 44956 – 12/54-12/62; 44957 – 12/54-12/62; 44967 – 3/57-1/63; 44968 – 5/54-12/62; 44970 – 5/57-9/64 & 6/65-9/65; 44995 – 12/54-1/56; 44996 – 12/54-1/63; 45007 – 2/50-7/50; 45010 – 2/50-3/51; 45011 – 2/50-7/50 & 5/54-5/55; 45112 – 11/51-5/52; 45119 – 5/54-12/54; 45214 – 8/51-12/54; 45281 – 11/51-9/53; 45396 – 5/54-12/54; 45400 – 11/51-12/54. Note the different tenders employed by the pair – riveted and welded. *C.J.B.Sanderson.*

Compare this view of former Ardrossan 2P No.40624 with the earlier view of classmate No.40649. This is Saturday 28th July 1962, the location is the rear of the coaling stage where, by now, condemned and redundant locomotives were being stored prior to being sold for scrap or hauled into Cowlairs for cutting up. This area of the shed had been used since LNER times for the storage of engines awaiting Cowlairs shops, be it for overhaul, or otherwise! It was an especially precarious time for steam locomotives during the early 60s' and the 4-4-0 was waiting to follow the latter course, a short trip to Cowlairs and oblivion which it duly took during the following month! *C.J.B.Sanderson.*

Another view of the 'dump' behind the coaling stage at Eastfield on the same August day in 1962; J39 No.64711 holds centre stage with other unidentified 0-6-0s behind. 2P No.40624 can be seen languishing in the background. The former Tweedmouth 0-6-0 had been condemned in May 1962 and is already vandalised somewhat prior to its eventual entry into Cowlairs for scrapping. Note the acres of allotments with what appear to be a number of new greenhouses amongst the potting sheds. *C.J.B.Sanderson.*

Staying on the east side of the depot, we see former Polmadie WD No.90060 looking rather desolate as it waits to enter Cowlairs for cutting up. The date is 1st March 1963 and the 2-8-0 had already been withdrawn at Polmadie during the previous June. A certain amount of cannibalisation has taken place, probably at 66A, to keep some other 'Austerity' in traffic. Formerly working on the Eastern Region, this WD was one of the 200 purchased by the LNER in 1945. It arrived at Polmadie on 25th February 1957 and other than a six month loan to Dawsholm later that year, it remained allocated to Polmadie throughout. It was believed that this particular engine was fitted with a boiler altered to the Scottish Region preference for the BR Standard type clack valves (see 90690) but, as can be seen, that was not the case and it obviously went for scrap with the original type of clack valve. *C.J.B.Sanderson.*

Seven months or so later and the WD 2-8-0 is long gone, its place now taken up by BR Standard Cl.4 2-6-4T No.80056. It is 20th October 1963 and not yet ten years old, the Cl.4 is laid up awaiting withdrawal. That decision was made in July of the following year but then No.80056 was re-instated in August, taken back to Polmadie and made ready (along with Nos.80125 and 80129) for transfer to Lostock Hall on the London Midland Region where such locomotives were still sought after. However, apparently, they were all three damaged during transit and just a couple of months later. On 10th October, No.80056, along with the other two Cl.4s, were condemned and then cut up at Crewe works in November. The 2-6-4T had gone into traffic at Polmadie on the 30th December 1954. In December 1962 it was transferred to Eastfield but was obviously surplus to requirements during 1963. Its external condition in this illustration indicates more than a few weeks in open storage. *C.J.B.Sanderson.*

In complete contrast to 80056! On the same day, and just a few yards away, another BR Standard Cl.4, Ardrossan's No.80000, shows off the results of a major overhaul which it received at nearby Cowlairs. It was amongst the last steam locomotives to receive such extensive (and expensive!) renovation because during the following April 1964, British Railways announced, by internal instruction, that all heavy overhauls were to cease forthwith. The following August authorisation was given whereby any locomotive 'requiring attention at works costing in excess of £1,000' would be withdrawn instead. In the summer of 1965 that figure was reduced to less than a half that amount - the end was certainly coming to meet steam locomotion head-on. This particular Cl.4 had spent all of its life working from sheds in south west Scotland – Ayr, Corkerhill, Hurlford, Corkerhill, Ardrossan, Corkerhill, in that order – and was continue to do so until withdrawn on New Years Eve 1966. Its eventual end also took place in Scotland, at Faslane. *C.J.B.Sanderson.*

1963 was also a bad time to be a steam locomotive with an ailment; if something was broken it was just as perilous but to have a major component like a broken cylinder, it certainly was the end! Such a catastrophe had befallen Gresley V2 No.60900 in April 1963 – the culprit is there before your very eyes – whilst working from St Margarets shed. It was condemned on 11th April and languished at 64A for a while before being dragged over to Eastfield from where entry to Cowlairs scrap yard would be regulated. This is the sorry looking 2-6-2 at the rear of Eastfield shed on 6th August 1963 waiting to continue its short journey to the breakers. Ten other V2s were broken up at Cowlairs, most being ex-St Margarets charges! Note the number, shed and works plates are all still in situ – some four months after the withdrawal of the V2. It would be nice to know what that piece of rope, tantalisingly secured to the front of the running plate on the right of the engine, was actually tied to. A similar situation on the left front reveals nothing. *David J.Dippie.*

Shortly after the ASLEF Strike had been brought to a conclusion, things started to get back to normality and such was the case on Saturday 25th June 1955 when this ex-Cowlairs K3 was brought onto Eastfield for its running-in routine to begin. No matter what their footplate colleagues were up to, the painters at Cowlairs kept their standards extremely high, including lining the cylinders. The St Margarets based 6MT 2-6-0 would no doubt make one or two runs over in the direction of its home shed during running-in but it would not be released back into 64A's care until 65A was satisfied with its performance and well-being. No.61924 had just completed a General overhaul (28th April to 25th June) which was to be its last, but a couple of Intermediate overhauls, one Light, one Heavy, would keep it in traffic for another five years up to its 20th December 1960 withdrawal. This view allows us to admire the Hamiltonhill line bridge from where so many of the Eastfield illustrations included in this album were captured. *C.J.B.Sanderson.*

As already mentioned, 1963 was a bad time for steam locomotives to start ailing in any fashion. Even if they had recently been fitted with the latest innovations – double blast pipe and chimney, smoke deflectors, AWS, etc. – they were still vulnerable if they were in the wrong place at the wrong time. This Gresley A3, No.60090, alongside the Eastfield coaling plant (where prospective inmates – short term and permanent – of Cowlairs gathered prior to entering the workshops) on 3rd November 1963 had recently been condemned at Eastfield even though its home shed was St Rollox! Now bathed in the light rain of an autumn shower, the Pacific is intact in every way except for its GRAND PARADE nameplates. Had they been removed at St Rollox shed, or even Eastfield; did Doncaster remove them when the A3 visited the 'Plant' works for a five week long Non-Classified repair, during the previous July and August? The quick answer was Eastfield where the plates were removed shortly after the A3 arrived from 65B on Saturday 19th October 1963. No.60090 had transferred to St Rollox shed in June 1962, from St Margarets, and was then transferred to Eastfield for a two week period – 31st December 1962 to 14th January 1963 – when it returned to St Rollox. However, the 65A transfer was purely on paper because the Pacific was actually in Doncaster shops from 19th November 1962 to 21st January 1963 undergoing a Casual Light repair (accident damage). Controversy had surrounded this locomotive since it was badly damaged in the Castle Cary accident in December 1937 but now it was about to make history again although not in such dramatic circumstances – it was to become the only A3 cut up at Cowlairs! *A.Dodgson.*

It wasn't all former LNER glamour passing through Eastfield en route to the scrapyard in 1963. Take a look at this Pacific. Former Polmadie 'Duchess' No.46227 has not only lost its DUCHESS OF DEVONSHIRE nameplates, along with its smokebox plates but its sense of direction appears to have left it too because Crewe was due south of 66A and at the time when this unusual scene was captured on film, the locomotive was due north of Polmadie! The answer lies in the fact that after withdrawal, the 'Duchess' was stored at Parkhead shed until it was moved to Eastfield during the week ending 2nd November 1963 to be prepared for onward transit to Crewe. Although one theory put forward was that perhaps the initial plan was to cut up the Pacific at Cowlairs! Anyway, No.46227 was sent to Carstairs the following week where it met up with sisters Nos.46231 and 46232 which had been in storage there. All three locomotives departed from Carstairs on 7th November destined for Crewe where our subject was broken up by Friday 29th November 1963. *I.W.Coulson.*

Having previously dealt with three Gresley locomotives in a row, another Gresley design with a difference would not go amiss. Former 1st Class Restaurant Kitchen car SC9021E stands in the middle of Eastfield's south yard in late 1963. It was actually chocked on a stub siding, complete with a pit beneath, radiating off the south yard turntable. The vehicle even had four seating sections for non-smokers but whether or not those instructions were adhered to at the time is unknown – perhaps unlikely. The carriage had been withdrawn from passenger service in 1961 and at some unknown date shortly afterwards, it was seconded by the CME to act as a mess room at Eastfield depot whilst rebuilding (complete renewal) of the shed was very slowly taking place. Apparently the carriage was in use at 65A until 1968 by which time it had been renumbered in the Departmental series: DE321067. For the odd LNER carriage (not 'coach' I'm reliably informed) aficionados amongst you, the subject vehicle was an LNER Diagram 11, built at Doncaster in 1934 and based on a Gresley design, to Order No.539. Its original number was 31849 but it was renumbered in 1943 under Thompson. What happened to the carriage after 1968 is unknown but I should imagine it would have been sold for scrap. *David.J.Dippie.*

The East Midlands branch of the Railway Correspondence & Travel Society used to organise an annual visit and tour of Scottish Region engine sheds, usually at about the Whitsuntide period every year. Whenever possible they used the same hostelries each time, and to keep everything nice and friendly, the same transport and driver. In 1958 the group required two vehicles – coach A and coach B being the designations – to ferry them about the country. We have pictures featuring one coach (A or B?) at Eastfield and another featuring a different coach (B or A?) at Polmont. Different members feature in the two illustrations, as do different drivers. However, Vic Forster features in both pictures which would be the way VF wanted it as he was the main instigator of these annual treks; and anyone who knew Vic, well....! One person who isn't on either photograph but was on the tour, was the photographer himself – F.W(Bill).Hampson. With the help of members of the RCTS East Midlands branch, and a surviving printed list of the travellers for the 1958 'mission' it has been possible to identify a number of those present, however we are still not totally sure of who is who. Nevertheless, the following list will, we hope, be of assistance to those who knew somebody on that particular trip:

Driver John Gilmour; Vic Forster; David Talkes; Keith Arnold; Peter Batty; Richard Bonser; Chris Boyle; Ken Clarke; J.R.Cook; John Fletcher; Les Folkard; John Foreman; Phil Fox; Peter Giddens; Peter Gray; R.De Hall, Bill Hampson; Don Harris; Chas Heywood; George Hebden; Ken Hunt; Norman Ling; Frank Lodge; Dave Loxley; Derek Middleton; Leonard Negus; John Proctor; Bob Ramsden; Ian Simpson; Michael Smith; John Smyth; Dave Swale; Lolly Taylor; R.S.Taylor; Peter Tozar; Tony Turner; T.Upshall; Bernard Vowles; John Wallbank; Maurice Waters; J.G.F.Winn; D.F.Zeidlar. Are you there too?

Taken on the same, albeit unrecorded, day that the former LNER carriage was captured on film, this breakdown crane would appear to be the only steam on shed at Eastfield. The Cowans Sheldon 45-ton capacity breakdown crane had been a permanent feature at Eastfield since 1940 when the LNER had acquired five other similar cranes for positioning at strategic depots up and down their system. Numbered initially 971588, the crane was renumbered RS1058/45 by British Railways – the match wagon was numbered 971589 and still carried that designation in this view. Stationed at Thornton Junction for the first month or so of its life, the crane was transferred to Eastfield to be out of range of German bombers but that was soon proved to be short sighted as Clydeside too suffered from bombing raids. However, the crane was there to stay. Even at twenty-odd years old, the appliance looks in good condition, no doubt its upkeep was a necessary requisite and, all important. *David.J.Dippie.*

A fine view of St Rollox shed yard on 5th April 1961 with three 'Class 5s' being the only engines outside the shed; from left to right they were Nos.44672 (Kingmoor), 45453 and 44998 (both Perth). Considering that St Rollox still had a considerable allocation of Stanier Cl.5s at this time (twenty-odd), besides ten of the BR Standard versions, it seems strange that none of those are accounted for amongst this trio but perhaps the 'locals' are lurking inside the shed. However, that was the nature of this shed with ex works engines rubbing shoulders with the daily inevitable arrivals from Perth especially. Most of the depot's twelve stabling roads are in view, a number not occupied but it was a Wednesday and most of the resident allocation would be out working. This former Caledonian engine shed was built in 1916 to replace a much smaller shed located near to the Locomotive works of the same name. A nearby junction, Balornock, lent its name to the new shed and over the ensuing decades the depot was known variously as Balornock or St Rollox. British Railways, and indeed local crews and shed staff tended to call the place St Rollox. The design of the building, with its adjacent repair shop (the high roofed end gable of which can be seen on the left), was to a CR standard and similar sheds could be found at Dalry Road, Grangemouth, and Polmadie when that shed was rebuilt by the LMS in 1925. The continuous smoke ventilator running from side to side of the roof was a BR addition which replaced the earlier single pots in about 1952. Ventilators were in fact one of the constants of engine shed roofs – they were constantly evolving from one design to the next and during a period of forty years or so, certain roofs were known to have had three or more different types of ventilator. *D.J.Dippie.*

35

Resident ex-Caley 2F No.57258 stands on the last (No.12) road at St Rollox on 14th May 1959. 65B still had about ten of these useful 0-6-0s for local freight and especially mineral workings but their time in service was coming to an end with some of the oldest members of the class already seventy-odd years old! Note the 12 designation on the wall to the left of centre, above the road; were they cast iron or carved timber? *I.W.Coulson.*

It is always nice to include a 'namer' or two and St Rollox had plenty to offer in the shape of its visitors; its own gaggle of 'namers' was restricted mainly to the handful of Cl.5s during much of the BR period but towards the end of its life, the shed attracted some exotic foreigners too. (*above*) This not quite exotic 'Jubilee' No.45673 KEPPEL, was a visitor from Perth in March 1953. The former LM Region engine was a newcomer to the Scottish Region having transferred from Preston to Kingmoor in September 1952. From Carlisle it moved to Perth during the following March. Note that it still has the Crewe-size figures on the cab side but that would change once St Rollox works got their hands on the 6P. (*below*) No.45715 INVINCIBLE was a Kingmoor engine, had been since 1936, and displays the typical St Rollox figures on the cabside in this May 1952 picture at virtually the same location in the shed yard; the tiny BR emblem did nothing to enhance the plain unlined tender. Only the cab appears to have any lining at all. *Both C.J.B.Sanderson.*

A splendid view of the manual coaling stage at St Rollox in August 1953 with ex-Caley 3P No.54483 having its fire cleaned. The 4-4-0 was allocated to Grangemouth shed at this time but in 1955 it would transfer to St Rollox where it would work out the rest of its days until withdrawal in July 1961. Behind, looking suitably 'booted and spurred' for the Oban road, with tablet exchange apparatus and miniature snowplough, is Cl.5 No.45155 – the one without a name – which was one of the St Rollox contingent numbered 45153 to 45159 of which four carried names. Note the 'spare' three-link coupling on the platform below the smokebox. The timber clad coal stage managed to 'exist' without any major rebuilding over its near fifty years of operation, neither subsidence nor tempest, having any effect. The small timber shed immediately above the 3P has a rather interesting balcony attached to its waist; could this have been an aid to cleaning those windows? In the early 20th Century such an appendage would be regarded as thoughtful, extravagant even in some circles, but in the 21st Century it would be condemned as unsafe because of its lack of a banister or guard rail. Nevertheless, from a modelling aspect it presents all sorts of opportunities. *C.J.B.Sanderson.*

Another of the St Rollox '5s' over the ash pit, and a namer too! No.45157 THE GLASGOW HIGHLANDER, also fitted out for working the Oban road, waits in line to visit the coaling stage in April 1953. Two of the St Rollox 'namers' Nos.45154 LANARKSHIRE YEOMANRY and 45156 AYRSHIRE YEOMANRY left Glasgow in April 1957 for pastures anew at Newton Heath in Manchester. Neither returned to Scotland and were still working from Lancashire sheds when withdrawn. To spoil the party completely for 65B, No.45155 departed for Edinburgh the following year. That engine too never went back and was withdrawn from Dalry Road shed in 1964. It is interesting to note that all of the coal wagons on the stage ramp are wooden bodied which, in 1953, was quite a spectacle as British Railways and its contractors were already well on the way to producing more than half of the eventual half million steel bodied mineral wagons it was to own. *C.J.B.Sanderson.*

The driver and fireman of Caprotti equipped Standard Cl.5 No.73149 take an interest in the photographer as their steed is turned on the St Rollox table on 4th May 1957. 65B had ten of these capable engines – 73145 to 73154 – acquired new during the first six months of 1957. When No.73149 was photographed, the final three had still to arrive from Derby. Our subject had been at St Rollox since late March and although only six weeks have passed since that time, the 4-6-0 has already lost its sheen. Why St Rollox shed was chosen to house this final batch of Caprotti engines is unknown, indeed the shed did not have any of the earlier 'normal' Standard 5s allocated, nor any of the Caprotti equipped Stanier Class 5s either. However, the depot was apparently short of Class 5s anyway, co-incidentally to the tune of about five engines, so that when the ten Standard 5s arrived, five Stanier 5s were transferred away. The new engines performed well on their designated work hauling the Glasgow (Buchanan Street)–Aberdeen express passenger services along with the Glasgow–Dundee workings. Our subject here was apparently regarded as the 'pick of the bunch' but their reign on the Aberdeen and Dundee routes was shortened by the advent of diesel locomotives not too many years later. The Type 2 diesels did not however have it all their own way because one particular class, the North British Loco. Co. contingent, tended to be somewhat unreliable. The Standards were anything but, even with an apparent lessening of maintenance, and they were still working the expresses in 1965 albeit in a filthy external condition. That was the last year that the ten St Rollox engines were still all together; three of them had gone by Christmas and 1966 saw six more withdrawn. The sole survivor from 1966, No.73146, lasted operationally until the end of steam on Scottish Region – 1st May 1967. That particular Standard was just ten years old at the time! *C.J.B.Sanderson.*

Whereas Eastfield shed took care of the ex works engines from Cowlairs, St Rollox (Balornock) engine shed looked after those which had attended St Rollox works. On 7th October 1961 Kingmoor based Stanier Cl.5 No.44958 was just ex-works the day before and was now carrying out various running-on turns prior to working home. Note J36 No.65297 buffered-up behind – contrasts galore between these two! *C.J.B.Sanderson.*

Another ex works subject was this Carstairs based Fairburn Cl.4 tank, No.42162, which, with an unidentified member of the same class, basks on the siding alongside the breakdown crane road at St Rollox in October 1956. The repair shop is to the right of the Cl.4 whilst at the rear of that was the machine shop topped by the depot's original water tank. Alongside that is the somewhat spidery-legged later addition, built to supplement the water supply in time for WWII. *C.J.B.Sanderson.*

It is amazing what a coat of paint and some careful lining can do to a locomotive's appearance. Fowler Cl.4 No.42417 (top) is seen on the shed yard on Saturday 28th October 1950 looking rather drab and plain. The Greenock Ladyburn based 2-6-4T normally worked on the south side of the Clyde between the coast and either Central or St Enoch termini but on this day a visit to St Rollox was necessary for reasons unknown. In total contrast (below) Dawsholm based Stanier Cl.3 tank No.40158 is in ex-works condition and has been superbly finished, even the wheel rims have been burnished. Note that No.40158 has a somewhat rural backdrop in this illustration, which was also captured on that October Saturday in 1950, long before the bank of Corporation flats were built on the north side of the shed. Both *C.J.B.Sanderson.*

Seen from a location across the main line from the depot, Inverness based 3P No.54493, somewhat work stained but obviously ex-works stands by the ash road at St Rollox in circa 1957. The Nissen hut was in use as the shed canteen at the time and jolly nice it looked too compared with the rest of the shed buildings. *C.J.B.Sanderson.*

A comparatively rare view of the rear end of a Gresley corridor tender, showing the open doorway, the porthole, and the knuckle coupling! The location is St Rollox shed (road number unknown) on Sunday 20th October 1963. The tender is No.5650, coupled to A4 No.60031 GOLDEN PLOVER, one of the regular performers on the 3-hour Aberdeen expresses and the Dundee trains, up to the Pacific's withdrawal in October 1965. To have a balanced diagram for the Aberdeen workings, St Rollox shed was obliged to have an A4 allocated and No.60031 was duly transferred from Haymarket on 3rd February 1962. Besides GOLDEN PLOVER, St Rollox also acquired No.60027 MERLIN on 20th May 1962 but it transferred back to former LNER territory at St Margarets nearly two-and-a-half years later in September 1964. Both however ended up in the same scrapyard at Shieldhall. *C.J.B.Sanderson.*

This undated – other than 1964 – view of Aberdeen Ferryhill A4 No.60026 MILES BEEVOR at St Rollox shows the Pacific reversing up to the coal stage whilst the fireman performs some acrobatics. Transferred from St Margarets to Ferryhill on 13th April 1964, the A4 would have started work on the 3-hour expresses shortly afterwards which gives us an idea of the date – post 13/4, by some margin. Why the big engine was visiting the coaling stage now, having apparently already turned is unknown. Perhaps a top-up was required? After withdrawal in December 1965, No.60026 was sold for scrap to a Motherwell firm but that sale was then cancelled by BR because certain 'parts' from the engine were required for sister No.60007. So, in the summer of 1966 No.60026 found itself at Crewe works of all places, being cannibalised! When the extraction of parts was completed the Pacific was then sold to a scrapyard in Blyth. *I.W.Coulson.*

Long before the A4s became regular performers on the 3-hour express workings from Aberdeen, Ferryhill used to supply its Peppercorn Pacifics for the passenger trains to Glasgow (Buchanan Street) too. On 15th March 1953 a nicely turned out A2, No.60531 BAHRAM is captured near the St Rollox the coal stage having arrived in Glasgow with a morning express from the Granite City. It was somewhat ironic that the diesel locomotives purchased by BR to take over from steam and work the Aberdeen passenger services became so unreliable that the LNER Pacifics, specifically the A4s, had to be introduced onto the expresses from 1962 onwards. Both the A2 and A4 classes benefited from the diesels' failure but if the Type 2 diesels had performed as planned, we probably would not have seen any former LNER Pacifics working after 1963, never mind into 1967! *C.J.B.Sanderson.*

The western aspect of a rebuilt Parkhead shed on Sunday 29th May 1955 with a 'full house' on show. Situated on the east side of Glasgow, north of the Clyde, the six-road through shed was opened by the NBR in February 1871. This view presents the shed in its rebuilt and final form after British Railways had installed a new roof, and a somewhat unique (for engine sheds) castellated style of gable; the east end was a mirror image. The main line, which was yet to be electrified, runs to the left of the shed, the distant signals denoting its path. After Dawsholm shed closed in October 1964, the four 'preserved engines' which had resided at 65D for some time, were brought here; Parkhead offering shelter to the quartet for another year before it too was closed. They moved on to Kipps which although closed, was still in use as a stabling point for diesel locomotives. *F.W.Hampson.*

A close-up of some of the resident engines on that Sunday 29th May 1955 with N2 No.69562 to the fore, along with a well replenished V1 No.67621. The N2s shared much the same duties as the V1s but apparently the 0-6-2T were not liked as much. *F.W.Hampson.*

This is Parkhead on Saturday 7th October 1961 with a dull overcast sky and a sense of gloom hanging over certain of the depot's steam residents. With the Glasgow 'Blue Trains' once again in business, the job of the numerous steam locomotives, gathered together to help out after the sudden and dramatic cessation of the new service twelve months previously, was finally finished. With the initial introduction of the electric services in November 1960, the V1s allocated to Parkhead were either laid-up or transferred away (to some strange places it might be added). However, a short time afterwards, when all the electric multiple units were withdrawn following some catastrophic and even life threatening incidents involving electrical equipment and passengers, steam motive power was once again called to the fore. No.67622 was one of those V1s which had answered the call. But the reprieve was only temporary and after twelve months working the local passenger services again, No.67622 was put into open store on 23rd September 1961. The lack of a chimney covering indicates that the 'storage' was simply a paper exercise, the authorities having no intention of resurrecting this or any other of the fourteen Parkhead based 2-6-2Ts again. Miraculously, a couple of the Parkhead V1s were put back into traffic, being sent away to sheds on the former Glasgow & South Western section but our subject was not one of them and it was condemned on 5th March 1962. After lying derelict for a further ten months, it was finally taken into Darlington for scrapping in January 1963. *C.J.B.Sanderson.*

Long before the electrification debacle and when the Gresley V1s reigned supreme on the local passenger services, No.67631 stands amongst the ash and clinker at Parkhead on Friday 16th September 1955. The reason for the V1's apparent cleanliness stems from the fact that it had only been back in traffic for nine weeks after a General overhaul at Darlington. A resident of Parkhead since being built at Doncaster in March 1935, this engine too went through virtually the same set of circumstances as No.67622 during its final few years of life: laid-off by electrification; called up when that failed; laid-off and stored November 1961 to 5th March 1962; condemned; taken away to Darlington for scrapping January 1963! *C.J.B.Sanderson.*

51

Parkhead's east end in 1959 with resident 4MTT N15 No.69190 playing second-fiddle to one of the favoured 350 h.p. diesel shunters of which the depot had seven examples allocated at this time. The following year a further nine new 0-6-0DE, ex BR workshops, were sent to Parkhead, and, at the same time, three 0-4-0 diesel hydraulics arrived from North British Loco. Co., to tackle the smaller jobs. The arrival of the second batch of 0-6-0DE – D3893 to D3901 – from Crewe in the summer of 1960 really did put paid to the N15s work and it was condemned on 16th August 1960, promptly taken off the premises to Inverurie works and cut up there in October. The 0-6-0DE population remained constant at sixteen locomotives but two of the 0-4-0DH transferred to Kipps shortly after delivery. However, even though the shed was still open, the diesel shunters did not stay 'on the books' at 65C and were instead transferred to Eastfield on 3rd November 1962, at least on paper, some three years before Parkhead was actually closed. *C.J.B.Sanderson.*

The Engine History Cards for the period in question simply state 'stored' but Eastfield D11/2s Nos.62681 CAPTAIN CRAIGENGELT and No.62672 BARON OF BRADWARDINE look more like they have been dumped at Parkhead on 19th August 1959. The tender of No.62680 LUCY ASHTON completes the trio of 65A 'Improved Directors' which were temporarily surplus to requirements! Apparently none of the three left this place except to go for scrap but that was some time off yet. Condemnation and the aftermath came fairly quickly compared with the waiting; Nos.62672 and 62681 went together on Thursday 13th July 1961, with No.62680 following on Friday 8th September! By co-incidence or otherwise, all three were cut up at the same location, Heatheryknowe, a former carriage and wagon works situated just a few miles to the east of Parkhead, on the line to Airdrie. That place was in use – with short bursts of activity followed by periods of quiet – from March 1961 to January 1962 and became responsible for scrapping twenty-four steam locomotives, amongst them five D11/2. Our illustrious but woebegone trio were dealt with between September and November 1961. *D.J.Dippie.*

The east end again, but some years later on Sunday 10th June 1962. B1 No.61117 is the focus of our cameraman and he was lucky to catch the 4-6-0 at Parkhead during that summer because the B1 transferred to St Margarets some nine weeks later on 13th August. In fact two other members of the 65C B1 allocation moved away to 64A on that 13th day of August also – Nos.61344 and 61404 – whilst the pair which remained behind – Nos.61067 and 61333 – were both condemned at the end of December 1962. *H.Forster.*

Tucked away in the north western suburbs of Glasgow, Dawsholm engine shed came into being in 1896 and comprised a six-road dead-end running shed with adjacent two-road repair shop. Initially its allocation comprised passenger tank engines in the main to handle the Caledonian's expanding network of passenger lines in and around Glasgow, especially the Low Level lines. As the decades passed, goods workings became the major factor for the depot's existence, Glaswegians tending to opt for the Corporation bus services rather than the train to carry them to and from work. The last class of locomotive allocated to Dawsholm for what might be termed 'passenger train duties' was the Stanier Class 3 2-6-2T of which No.40176 was one of nine which came to the shed in December 1939. Another arrived in May 1940 and finally at the start of the BR period two more arrived. Not all of the nine early transfers stayed at Dawsholm continuously although at least three never moved away until their withdrawal in December 1962. Of the others, they moved around the former LMS sheds in Scotland but nearly always returned to Dawsholm. In this October 1957 view of No.40176, the 3P is standing near to the shed throat, probably ready to visit the coaling stage. Recently ex-works, this engine is wearing the new BR crest but on this side it is displaying one of the wrong-faced versions. *C.J.B.Sanderson.*

55

In late October 1950 when the former North British two-road engine shed at Stobcross was closed, its allocation of seven N15 0-6-2Ts, which had been sub-shedded from Eastfield, were transferred onto the allocation of nearby Dawsholm so that they could carry on their usual daily workload taking goods trains in and out of Glasgow docks. Nationalisation had enabled BR to close facilities such as the ex-LNER shed at Stobcross and move engines to a convenient and nearby former LMS depot without too much rearrangement of workings and crew rosters. The useful and powerful six-coupled tanks remained a fixture at Dawsholm for the rest of the decade and in 1957 a couple more of the class arrived in exchange for two which had transferred away. Besides Dawsholm, other ex-LMS sheds in the Glasgow area – Polmadie, St Rollox and even Motherwell – had one or more of these tank engines 'on the books' at some time during the Fifties. This is one of the seven, No.69163, highlighted by the few rays of the late afternoon sun at Dawsholm on 8th March 1952. Although its external appearance is no too bad compared with many at this time, No.69163 was soon to enter Cowlairs for a General overhaul. Approximately halfway through its sojourn at 65B, the forty-year old tank would eventually return to the Eastfield fold in May 1954 and from where it would be operational for another eight years before withdrawal. Note the shunters' step below, and the handrail attached to, the bunker; useful appendages for the shunting staff when trains were being assembled in the various yards served by these engines. *C.J.B.Sanderson.*

Another former LNER tank engine which found itself at Dawsholm shed was J88 No.68336 which had transferred from Kipps in October 1960. It wasn't the first of its class to grace the former Caley shed, because, on 29th October 1950 when the Stobcross N15s moved to 65D, one of the little J88s which was also resident at the closing ex-NBR shed, No.68333, transferred with them; it stayed at Dawsholm until condemned in March 1958. It was immediately replaced by No.68344 which was itself replaced by our subject, albeit some three months after No.68344's departure to Grangemouth. The reason for Dawsholm housing these diminutive tank engines was much the same as the reason for having the N15s allocated, although trip working was not their speciality; shunting the installations at Glasgow's dock was! Another of the dumb-buffered tanks, No.68331 had been on loan to Dawsholm for a week in January 1955 prior to settling in at Yoker. Both Nos.68336 and 68344 had spent time at Motherwell prior to joining the 65D stud. In this view captured by the sand store at Dawsholm on 8th September 1962, No.68336 had already been withdrawn for more than three months and was to remain here for another nine until being sold for scrap the following summer. Note the old BR emblem which was affixed at the 0-6-0Ts last works visit in April 1956, a year before the new BR crest was unveiled. *C.J.B.Sanderson.*

During the 1960s Dawsholm became the temporary home for what could be described as the pride of Scottish pre-Group motive power. Known by the staff at Dawsholm as the 'vintage engines,' the engines in question were often called upon for railtour duties prior to their installation in the Glasgow Museum of Transport. They were of course the Caledonian 'Single' No.123, the Highland Railway 4-6-0 No.103, the North British 4-4-0 No.256 GLEN DOUGLAS, and the youngster of the bunch, and only just into its Forties by then, the former Great North of Scotland 4-4-0 No.49 GORDON HIGHLANDER. Here, inside the shed on 5th April 1961, the quartet, ranged in pairs, are inspected by the father of the photographer. Even in the grimy, dark and soot laden surroundings of the building, the four preserved locomotives still shone. Apparently, according to A.G.Dunbar, a professional railwayman and lifelong enthusiast, the staff appointed to care for these engines looked after them with an intensity which could be placed in the 'loving' category! Note not just the painted mudguards but the buffer heads on No.123. How that effect was accomplished is unknown but whoever thought of that particular touch should be congratulated – pure Victorian. *D.J.Dippie.*

In complete contrast to the 'preserved four' we have this Ivatt Class 4 which is not doing a lot to enhance BR's image. Nick named 'Flying Pigs' – for reasons unknown – the engine appears to be trying its best to become as dirty as possible before either a call to works or withdrawal, whichever comes first! The date is 6th August 1963, a Tuesday, and No.43136 is stabled at the north end of the yard in late afternoon. By the end of the month instructions will have been issued whereby Dawsholm was to send this, and its other two Ivatt Class 4s, Nos.43135 and 43140, to the North Eastern Region in a prelude to winding down the depot's duties but in their place ScR, including Dawsholm, was to receive six of the BR Standard Cl.4s from the NER. All three of the Ivatt 2-6-0s had been allocated to Dawsholm during September and October 1961 and had come from other Scottish Region depots. The trio were originally part of a batch sent new to the Region between July and December 1951 – Nos.43132 to 43141 – which at that time were sent mainly to Eastfield. Over the intervening dozen years between their appearance and eventual transfer to the NER in September 1963, the Scottish contingent managed to serve at no less than fourteen depots between them; these ranged from Perth to Carlisle Canal and most places in between. Keeping diversification in mind, the Dawsholm three all went their separate ways when they left Scottish Region; No.43135 went to Thornaby, 43136 to Ardsley, and 43140 to West Auckland. Seeing that a BR Standard tender is visible in the frame, it is worth recounting that one of the Cl.3 2-6-0s, No.77005, had a brief stay at 65D in March 1954 prior to moving on to Hamilton. But now see next. *D.J.Dippie.*

BR Standard Cl.4 No.76100 arrived brand new at Dawsholm from Doncaster works in May 1957. It was quickly followed by Nos.76101 to 76103. Being classified as mixed traffic, that is exactly what Dawsholm shed employed the 2-6-0s for. This is No.76100 in June 1957 having lost its ex-works sparkle, after a month of work. Although three of the four transferred to other depots at one time or another, they all returned to 65D. In October and November 1963, as part of an unequal swap (see previous caption) with the North Eastern Region, Dawsholm received two more Standard Cl.4s – Nos.76046 and 76074, the latter taking the place of the last departing WD 2-8-0 from Dawsholm, No.90489. The six Standard Cl.4s were still at Dawsholm when the shed was finally got ready for its closure on Monday 5th October 1964 but when that day arrived, all six had moved on to further duties at Grangemouth. 65D was demolished and all trace disappeared beneath a road scheme. *C.J.B.Sanderson.*

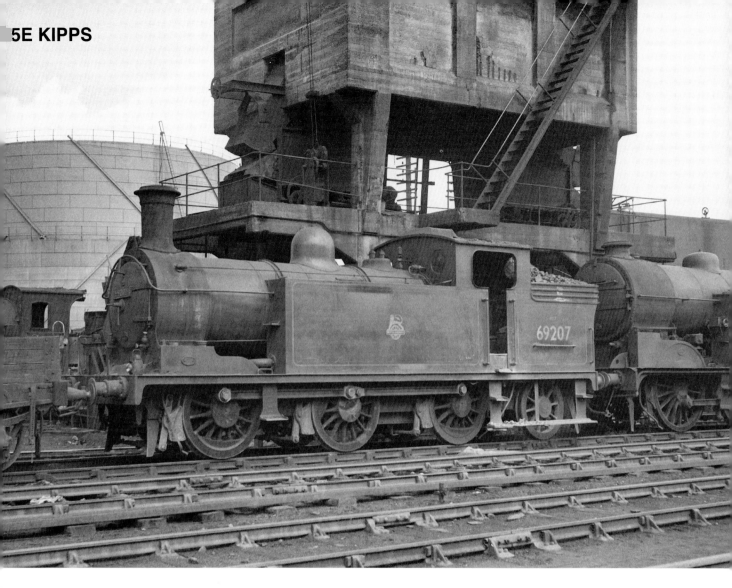

N15 No.69207 stables beneath the coaling plant on 27th April 1958; N2 No.69518 stands behind. With a large gasworks on its northern boundary, Kipps engine shed had a permanent and somewhat unmistakable 'aroma' about the place. This depot was about as far away from the country idyll that it was possible to be! The number of locomotives allocated to Kipps during BR days usually stood at around fifty engines and consisted six-coupled tender engines for hauling mineral trains, half a dozen N2 tanks for the passenger workings, supplemented by an equal number of V1s, and a collection of shunting tanks, ranging from the diminutive Y9s to these sturdy N15s. *C.J.B.Sanderson.*

Same engine, same location, two years apart. (top) Resident Y9 No.68110 stables beneath the coaler in 1959 coupled to its normal type of coal carrier which had long been converted from an open wagon. *C.J.B.Sanderson*. On 21st May 1961 (bottom) the engine, in its usual filthy state, now has a different coal carrier which appears to have been rapidly fashioned from a later model of five-plank open wagon. Neither vehicle is identifiable numerically, but both carry the MP designation on the left corner, adjacent to the engine. The shunters, it will be noted, have also been accommodated with steps and handrails. Note that the top carrier carries the legend Celtic whilst the lower one appears to be somewhat bent. *F.W.Hampson*.

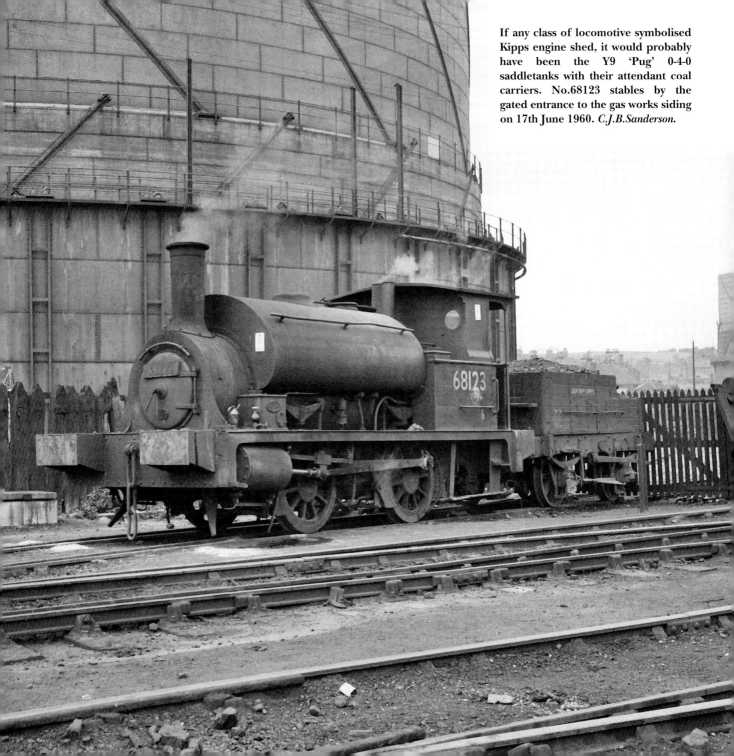

If any class of locomotive symbolised Kipps engine shed, it would probably have been the Y9 'Pug' 0-4-0 saddletanks with their attendant coal carriers. No.68123 stables by the gated entrance to the gas works siding on 17th June 1960. *C.J.B.Sanderson.*

The history of locomotive facilities being made available at Kipps goes back to 1837 when the Monklands & Kirkintilloch Railway provided a one-road engine shed which apparently survived until it was burnt down in 1890! That date coincides with the opening of the three-road shed in this view which, on Sunday 10th June 1962, was getting towards the end of its life, particularly as a building to house steam locomotives. Kipps closed to steam during January of the following year but it remained open for stabling diesels until November 1967 when a new stabling point was brought into use and 65E was allowed to lay derelict for some time afterwards. Many of the steam engines in this view were redundant, the growing diesel shunter fleet – one of the seven 350 h.p. 0-6-0DE types allocated to Kipps at this time (there had been eleven of them once, the first arriving 26th November 1957, ex Eastfield) can be seen poking its nose out of the shed; an English Electric Type 1 D8113 was lurking, out of view, near the office/amenities block. As a sort of replacement for the 'Pugs' four of the 0-4-0DH shunters arrived between September 1960 and September 1962. In September 1967 a visit by enthusiasts found two 0-4-0DH shunters on shed along with seven 0-6-0DE types. Stored were four of the by now infamous NBL Bo-Bo main line diesels which appeared to have been in a sorry state, having been cannibalised or vandalised! *H.Forster.*

Not quite in the engine shed but not too far away and certainly worth a look. Tucked away in one of the wagon repair shops at Kipps on 21st May 1961 was one of the strangest locomotives ever to have graced the metals of this former North British Railway stronghold – and possibly Scotland at that time. The vehicle was the Metropolitan-Vickers 2,500 h.p. prototype 25kV a.c. A1A-A1A E2001. The reason for the 109-ton locomotives' presence in the Central Belt is unknown but probably the recent electrification of the Glasgow area suburban lines had something to do with it. Judging from its external appearance, the 'leccy' had not moved for a while and during the three years since its conversion from a gas turbine (as 18100) to pure electric (E1000), it had only been involved with testing and training, never apparently having hauled a revenue earning train. It would be interesting to know the when and why it came to Scotland, and when it actually departed and where to! *H.Forster.*

Beetlecrusher in residence! Grangemouth Fouldubs engine shed actually had two of these former Caledonian 2F 0-6-0T as residents during BR days: Nos.56152 and 56164. Our subject, looking none too clean but luckily having a readable smokebox numberplate, is seen inside the shed on Thursday 5th August 1954, exactly one year before transfer to Eastfield, its work at Grangemouth having been taken over by one of the growing fleet of 350 h.p. 0-6-0DE shunters. The latter of the pair remained at 65F until August 1958 when it was transferred to St Rollox and promptly withdrawn within a few weeks of arrival at 65B. Behind the 0-6-0T, the depot's solitary ex-CR 2P 0-4-4T No.55238 receives attention from fitters. *F.W.Hampson.*

On a running-in turn after attention at Cowlairs works, Speke Junction's Stanier Cl.5 No.45386 stables out in the yard at Grangemouth on 16th May 1964. This class was no stranger to Grangemouth and no less than twenty had been allocated over the BR years; the LMS seems to have deprived the shed of the type completely. The earliest examples arrived in April and July 1948, the first, No.44967 moving on in June; No.45468 however remained at the shed until November 1949 along with No.45355. Thereafter, the allocation of Class 5s was somewhat sporadic with No.45119 representing the class from September 1951 until May 1954. During that period No.45396 arrived in August 1951, then Nos.45011 and 45013 came in March 1952 but the latter engine transferred away during the following September; 45011 and 45396 moved away in May 1954. That then was the start of a lean period which did not end until September 1960 when Nos.45177 and 45178 transferred in. From thereon, until closure of the depot to steam, in October 1965, the Stanier 5s kept coming – some thirteen engines came on a regular basis and six of those were eventually withdrawn at 65F whilst the five which survived until the end at Grangemouth, went on to pastures anew elsewhere. *A.Ives.*

WD 2-10-0 No.90755 simmers on the 70ft turntable at a date unknown but believed to be circa June 1950 before the big 'Austerity' received a smokebox numberplate; it appears that the tender is without any markings too but there may well have been a BR emblem beneath that coating of grime. The turntable for this shed was provided as far back as 1907, basically for the opening of the depot, but the vacuum tractor was not fitted until 1946 – just in time to handle these monsters! Note that the vacuum hose is not connected to the engine so the 2-10-0 was possibly just arriving on the table to be turned. No.90755 actually arrived at Grangemouth in February 1949 as WD No.73779 and was renumbered during the following April. A smokebox numberplate was eventually fitted during a prolonged Heavy General overhaul at Cowlairs which lasted from 13th December 1950 to 25th April 1951! This WD spent the whole of its Scottish Region life working from Grangemouth shed and of the other eleven class members which had been allocated to Grangemouth up to the end of the class, only one other remained at 65F throughout – 90765. Besides the 2-10-0 version of the 'Austerity' Grangemouth also housed seventeen of the 2-8-0 version over the years between June 1949 and December 1965. This view offers a glimpse of the one-road repair shop with its roof glazing and continuous ventilator. When the shed was built the repair shop was equipped with a 40-ton hoist not quite enough strength to handle one of these but ideal for all the Caley six-coupled goods engines which had been allocated over the decades. No.90755 was withdrawn on 29th December 1962, a date when the remaining members of the class were also condemned. They had been useful engines at least as far as Fouldubs engine shed was concerned. *C.J.B.Sanderson.*

Just a month out from a Heavy General overhaul, WD 2-8-0 No.90560 looks almost respectable in this photograph captured on the north side of the shed yard on 28th April 1963. A newcomer to the Grangemouth allocation during the previous December, this 'Austerity' was to stay at the shed until the end of steam at 65F and transferred away to Dunfermline on 21st October 1965. As mentioned in the previous caption, the 2-8-0 WD outnumbered the 2-10-0 version but their presence at the shed, unlike the larger engine, was not continuous throughout. During the period from April 1952 until October 1955, some two and a half years, there was not one of the class 'on the books' at 65F. In the right background we can just glimpse the diesel fuel tanks inside their protective bund wall; they were to become quite busy over the following decades. *C.J.B.Sanderson.*

Finally, we present the Grangemouth breakdown assets as at June 1950. As can be seen, this hand-me-down from goodness knows where consisted a former Glasgow & South Western six-wheel passenger vehicle which at one time had corridor connections but by now had changed somewhat from its original condition. What, for instance did that roof layout signify? Its fleet number appears to be M191482. A real vintage piece but how much was actually original? Answers on a postcard.......! *C.J.B.Sanderson.*

Initially Fort William shed was placed in the '63' Perth District as 63D but in May 1955 it became part of the '65' Eastfield District as 65J. However, five years later it returned to the Perth District as 63B, 'promoted' at the expense of Stirling which had in fact closed, hence the return to the fold! A decade later, during the days when diesels ruled, in July 1970, Perth depot closed and Fort William had to revert back to the Eastfield District, this time as 65H. In May 1973 BR dropped its number and letter shed coding in favour of a two-letter code based loosely on the initial letter of the depot name and one other, usually the first letter of the next syllable or second section of the name. Fort William naturally became FW. In this glorious view, captured on film on Saturday 5th May 1956, Fort William was well and truly 65J and K2 No.61787 LOCH QUOICH carries the new code on its shed plate. Note the 'standing room only' situation at the shed, around which are engines of both LNER and LMS origin. The allocation at this time consisted mainly of former LNER classes, K1, K2, and J36 but change was constant at this outpost. The named K4s which had been allocated at the start of the decade had moved to Eastfield in June 1954 but were still regular visitors on passenger workings from Queen Street. Their place had been taken by the Peppercorn K1s Nos.61997, 62031, 62034 and 62052; two others had preceded them in June 1952 – Nos.62011 and 62012. Perhaps the most noticeable motive power changes involved the appearance of former LMS locomotives during May 1954 in the shape of the Stanier Class 5s, courtesy of the shed being in the Perth District at that time. Six of the 4-6-0s arrived at 63D but were all gone by December of that year. However the disappearance of one lot brought another batch of half a dozen to the depot and these were there for the long term, or at least until the shed was closed to steam in 1962. *C.J.B.Sanderson.*

A regular occurrence at Fort William shed was the turning of the observation coach which was coupled to the rear of certain passenger trains. In the presence of a B1, K4 and a Cl.5, one of the J36 is pushing the coach onto the table ready for the 180 degree turn on 18th June 1960. Vacuum stored in the tanks on each side of the table will be able to power a tractor which would turn the vehicle in the absence of motive power. Once the deed is completed, the J36 will ride onto the table, couple up to the observation coach and take it back to the station. *I.Falcus.*